the WOO of POO

CHANGE YOUR LIFE IN THE TIME YOU TAKE A SH*T

POO~POURRI

𝓉𝒽𝑒 WOO* OF POO

Printed in China
ISBN: 978-0-692-90429-9
First edition: October 2017
Published by No. 2 Productions
A division of Scentsible, LLC

Art Directed by Nicole Story and Lindsey Bellanti
Designed by Allie Hill, Melissa Harrison, Brandon Nickerson
Illustrations by Christina Mrozik

In some circles (ones full of Powerpoint slides and acronyms), WOO means Winning Others Over. In the world of Shakespeare's sonnets, the word "woo" can mean that you are trying to charm the pants off of your lover. "Whom thine eyes woo as mine importune thee..."

At Poo-Pourri, we encourage the use of both of these definitions of woo. But for us, woo is short for woo-woo. You know, woo-woo—all the cosmic-y, new age-y mumbo jumbo that we love to dive into whether there's scientific evidence to back it up or not. In short, woo is magic. It's our ridiculously fun belief in the impossible and the unknown. It's the secret to our success. And yours as well.

this book is dedicated
to all the doers and dreamers
and no inbetweeners.

table of CONTENTS

– FOREWORD –

HISTORY OF poo~ POURRI

2007 After 9 months of formulating *(and hundred of smell tests)*, Suzy Batiz invents Poo-Pourri

2008 Sales reach $1 million strictly by word of mouth

2010 The Poo Crew grows to a whopping 10 employees

2013 Poo-Pourri earns the Good Housekeeping Seal by passing all of their tests *(wish we could say the same for 9th grade algebra. Sorry, Mom)*

YouTube video *"Girls Don't Poop"* goes viral with 10 million views in 2 weeks. Poo-Pourri has millions of dollars in backorders and the company almost goes under. *Yikes!*

2014 International distribution grows to over 90 countries—*World Poo domination commence*

"Girls Don't Poop" video wins a Webby Award and AdAge's "Funniest Viral Video of the Year"

Suzy is awarded an Edison Award for creating one of the most innovative products in the world *(and she meets Elon Musk!)*

2016 "Will the Real Suzy Batiz Please Stand Up?" Suzy stars with Betty White on ABC's *To Tell the Truth*

Poo-Pourri realizes it's pretty *badass* at this whole video thing and launches in-house production company, *No. 2 Productions*

Poo-Pourri videos hit 250 million total views

2017 The Poo Crew grows to 75 employees *(growing pains are real)*

25 million bottles sold...and counting. That's a lot of stink-free flushes. *You're welcome, Earth!*

Poo-Pourri celebrates its 10-year anniversary by writing *The Woo of Poo* (this is kind of an *Inception* moment, huh?)

A WORD OR poo FROM SUZY

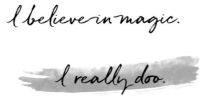

I believe in magic.

I really doo.

You might not expect to hear this from a CEO of a multimillion-dollar business, but it's true. I believe in magic with all of my heart. My own very improbable life and the fact that Poo~Pourri Before-You-Go Toilet Spray is a thriving business prove that magic is afoot. After all, my story simply just doesn't add up on (toilet) paper otherwise. None of it should have worked. But somehow it did. And that somehow was magic.

Now, you might be wondering, "Suzy, when you say 'magic,' you're being all cute and metaphorical, right? Certainly a businesswoman and mother of three grown children, who's bootstrapped her own company debt-free from her kitchen into the hearts of millions of consumers, doesn't believe in, um, magic. You must mean 'personal growth' or perhaps you're using a cheesy business acronym like Managerial Access Grows Individual Competence. Surely, you don't mean 'magic magic?' That's just a little too woo-woo to wrap my head around."

Let me be clear. When I say "magic" I do indeed mean "magic magic." Magic, as defined by the *Oxford English Dictionary*, is:

MAG·IC

noun

1. the power of apparently influencing the course of events by using mysterious or supernatural forces

adjective

1. having or apparently having supernatural powers.
2. wonderful; exciting

verb

1. move, change or create by or as if by magic

I get it. It's hard to believe in magic because we've been taught that anything worth having should be hard and full of struggle. And while there are enough hardships and tragedies to go around, there is also an infinite amount of wonder and love that is your birthright. The Universe is an ultimately supportive place.

Think about it: We orbit a terrifying nuclear inferno, basking in its radiation every day, and even the biggest skeptics on our planet call this radiation "sunshine!" We are here to tell you that the essence of this cosmos is to support life—your life. This is a truth that can't be argued. Even now, science can't fully understand or explain it. And, well, that's pretty magical!

It's why we wrote this book. At Poo~Pourri, we've seen what The Woo of Poo can do for our lives and our business. Yes, magic is hard to see or smell. And things this amazing are even harder to believe in sometimes. The Woo is there, waiting for you to feel it. It is waiting to support your dreams. But serendipity isn't just something that happens to you. It's something you practice. That's how you let The Woo of Poo in, and this woo-woo magical thinking can change your life.

So if you're open to something badass and exciting, if you want to influence the course of your life events in mysterious and naturally supernatural ways, then this is the book for you. If you're a hard-nosed skeptic who's looking to IPO her start-up and retire at 30, then this is also the book for you. The Woo of Poo is real whether you believe in it or not.

That's how magic works. I should know.

GREETINGS FROM THE *poo* CREW

Hello.

Welcome to our little Poo book.

We've got lots of stories to tell you. Ones that will change your life in the time it takes to go number two. So make sure the seat is down, drop your drawers and let it rip. After all, it's our job to help you transform this everyday shituation into one of wonder, fascination and maybe even illumination (if you push hard enough).

we are the employees of poo~pourri...
a.k.a. the poo crew

Yes, we are proud professionals who have the word "Poo" permanently emblazoned on our LinkedIn profiles, and we like to brag about this. A lot. We are the people you will meet at Fourth of July picnics who will gladly tell you that we work for Poo~Pourri, the world's best Before-You-Go Toilet Spray. You know the funny videos you've seen on YouTube? The ones with the British redhead in the blue dress on a toilet? Yeah, that's us. We turn crappy into happy.

And we do all of this because we believe in Suzy's audacious dream. We believe in eating chaos for breakfast and pooping out epic shit by noon. We believe in defying outmoded, limiting beliefs—like "girls don't poop."

We believe in dismantling systems that make people ashamed of a natural digestive process. We believe in transforming stinky situations and odors into uplifting, even funny, moments. And because we have followed Suzy on this wild journey, we have liberated millions of people from the unnecessary anxiety and embarrassment of pooping in public restrooms, and we've done so without harsh chemicals or fake smells.

And somewhere along the way, Poo~Pourri has changed us as well—in dramatic and amazing ways! Seriously. It's what we call "The Woo of Poo." There is a certain magic that happens when you work at Poo~Pourri. You are asked to confront your dreams, follow your instincts and open your soul to unseen possibilities.

We realize that this is not normal. However, we believe from the bottom of our butts that it should be. Besides, being normal is kind of boring and perhaps not the fastest path to greatness.

Trying to be normal never got Janis Joplin, Nikola Tesla or Marie Curie anywhere. They were woo-woo well before everyone started drinking kombucha and hanging dreamcatchers on their walls. They did and said things that freaked all of their co-workers out while ultimately inspiring the rest of us.

Woo and inspiration are two sides of the same coin. You go looking for one, you will surely find the other. At Poo~Pourri, we encourage everyone to dive—no, cannonball—into their own weirdness. The water's great, by the way.

We've gathered up our Woos to help you co-create and transform your life in a way that only Poo~Pourri can. We wrote this little book for you to read while dropping your daily deuce, while laying a brick, while owning the throne. So take your time. Read it one small, digestible tip at a time or read it all at once.*

The quantum power of The Woo of Poo unfolds however you'd like to make it happen.

Disclaimer: Should you choose to go for the gastric gold and read the entire book in one shitting, we cannot be held responsible for any leg or butt numbness that occurs. Though, we do recommend toilet yoga. Google it.

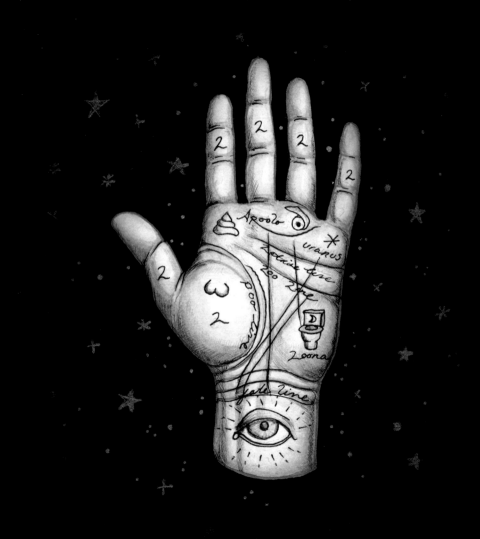

RELAX AND
unclench

K\AY, let's get sharted—sorry, started. But first, you are going to have to understand that jumping into The Woo of Poo is going to be unlike diving into any book you have ever read.

It's about thinking thoughts you have never thought before. It's about seeing through the illusions that hold you back. So we are going to go places where most books are too scared to go:

Like your sphincter.

Yep, you read that correctly.

we are going to start at your bottom.

Ever wonder why certain parts of your body, like your sphincter, are off-limits in day-to-day conversation? Ever ponder why you might feel shame admitting that you even poop? Where does this shame come from?

This is a useful question to ask. Ask it every time you encounter shame. Ask it right now about your own sphincter and other body parts you might be too nervous to even mention.

We get it. Words have meaning. And there is indeed a time and place for every conversation. But most people have forgotten that we get to choose the texture and meaning we give to the words we use. We are the ones who actually attach the shame to the body parts that these words represent. And with this shame about our bodies come limits to how we lead our lives. Shame in general is bad for children and other living things—like you and me.

So why exactly is pooping such a source of embarrassment, shame and vulnerability? No judgment. Tell us how you really feel. Magic teachings always say this: If you can name it, you can claim it. So name your feelings, so that you can claim them.

When did you first feel ashamed of going number two in a shared bathroom? What adjustments to your day do you make to hide from this shit shame? And how's that working out for you?

Okay, now that we have hopefully gotten you out of your comfort zone a little, you might notice that you are somewhat tense. So now we want you to actually focus on how your sphincter feels, your root chakra.

with your mind, locate your sphincter.

BODY
CHAKRAS

IT ALL STARTS AT THE
bottom

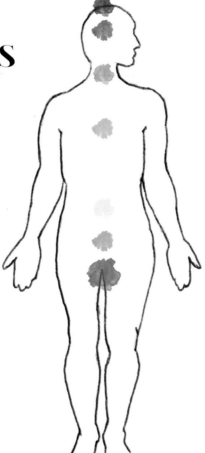

- ● CROWN
- ● BROW
- ● THROAT
- ● HEART
- ● SOLAR PLEXUS
- ● SACRAL
- ● *root*

Notice the tension level in your root chakra, the Muladhara. It rules your first three vertebrae, your bladder and your colon. When this chakra is open, you feel safe and fearless.

So take a deep cleansing breath all the way down to your belly and relax your Muladhara—or, as you probably refer to it, your "butthole." Chances are, you have been clenching it tight all day and didn't even realize it. That's what we do. We clench our bumholes in order to feel in control of life, and by the end of our day, we are a ball of knots and held-in stress.

Take a deep breath again.
Tighten your buttocks and then let go.
Deep. Cleansing. Breath.
Aaaaaahh...

Notice how relaxing your balloon knot and breathing relaxes your shoulders and your neck. Notice how your brow and jaw muscles loosen. Notice how all the tension melts away in your body as you breathe and relax your nether regions. You're welcome.

Unclenching your sphincter is a ninja move to relax your whole body quickly. You can do this little trick and no one will be any the wiser. We recommend unclenching your starfish a few times a day. Just breathe...clench and unclench. In traffic. In business meetings. When you are talking to your asshole boss (pun intended).

A
MIND
IS LIKE A
parachute...

IT DOES NOT
WORK
IF IT IS NOT
open.

- FRANK ZAPPA

Remember:

relax your hole → relax your whole

It's the most hidden part of our body language. Your visible anatomy might seem open, but if your sphincter is closed, you are secretly not open to what is being offered. Recognize this feeling. We clench our buttholes to stay in control, to resist. It makes us rigid in our thinking. It makes us unwelcoming to change.

we call people "tight-asses" for a reason.

Words do indeed have meaning.

Learning to keep this muscle group relaxed allows you to move more freely, feel more authentically, be open to new ideas and move into a state of flow more easily. If you are going to really ingest the juicy ideas in The Woo of Poo, you are going to have to be wide open.

What is openness, exactly? It's a state of being receptive, of being bright-eyed and ready to explore a world of new ideas. It's the exact opposite of being a tight-ass.

Openness is actually an inborn temperament and personality trait that has been investigated by evolutionary biologists and psychologists for years. The current theory is that humans, like most mammals, evolved this trait because it was beneficial to procreation and, therefore, their evolution. Mammals that were open to new ideas, food sources and environments progressed. The ones who weren't didn't.

Human openness has led our species to traversing continents of a once flat planet, accepting the laws of gravity despite religious doctrines and understanding that poxes aren't spread by angry witches. Openness has been, and continues to be, essential to moving the human race forward. Your ancestors had the open trait—you are here.

So if you count yourself as a part of this race, you might want to practice being a lot more open. Even if your annoying relative keeps posting crappy political rants on Facebook that even Poo~Pourri can't cover up.

When this happens:
Just breathe.
Fill up with air all the way to your belly.
Clench and unclench your donut hole.
Exhale.

Repeat.

At Poo~Pourri, we never do things half-assed—we always use our whole ass (and then some). So we aren't just open. We are OPEN TO OPENNESS. We know that all belief systems have their place in life. We try to be brave enough to not take life, or its "truths" too seriously. So we practice outrageous openness to all stories, ideas, beliefs and dreams.

what the flush does that even mean, right?

Well, it means we embrace everything and dismiss nothing. We are open to infinite possibilities, which means it's just as possible to be right as it is to be wrong. Good news is being right or wrong doesn't really matter when you are creating flow or love. In fact, it kind of gets in the way.

So with this freedom and curiosity, we explore all limits. This means we get into everything: hard science, Jazzercise, shamanic practice, fluid dynamics, vision boards, TED, CrossFit, aromatherapy, sonic resonance, sacral massage, yoga, group colonics. (Okay, just kidding about the group colonics, but we probably would…)

We have been known to call a psychic about how to increase sales. We've hired a feng shui consultant to auspiciously rearrange our office so everyone flows and collaborates better. We sage our conference room after super-tense meetings. We consult our hipster oracle cards that we keep on display atop our desks. We get all contracts signed before Mercury goes retrograde. Anyone who has done business with Poo~Pourri knows we are serious about our woo-woo.

The woo-woo fringe is where all the best ideas are hooking up and birthing new ideas. As a creative company, we believe it's our job to bring these babies home—to nurture them into million-dollar missions that grow into billion-dollar world changers. Quite frankly, if we aren't being a little woo-woo, then we aren't doing our jobs at Poo~Pourri.

Look, you don't even have to believe in astrology or feng shui or psychics or any of that shit to benefit from consulting them on behalf of your ideas.

It's the sheer act of asking the question to the Universe in a way that excites you, which provokes a great answer. When we ask questions of a completely unorthodox or random source, it gives us radically different answers than people who insist on consulting more orthodox experts or models, or who simply never ask the questions.

Being a little woo-woo will stimulate your brain in ways you have yet to imagine. It will spark hysterical conversations, raucous synchronicity and infectious collaboration! So loosen up. Relax that sphincter and try exploring something that's a little freaky-deaky. It will rock your world.

SUZY SAYS: *loosen up.* Life's too important to be taken so seriously.

TAKE A
SHIFT
exercise

Here are some reflections
to help you shift your mindset
from closed to *open*.

1. What person or idea annoys you the most?

2. How are you actually similar to that person? Or what about this idea threatens you?

3. What is it about this person or idea that really grinds your gears?

4. Could you ever see how someone could believe such a thing? If so, how does this happen?

5. When you are faced with something you don't agree with, try not to argue your side. Instead, try being curious. In fact, phrase your next sentence to the person as "I am curious as to why" or "Help me understand why" instead of arguing your point of view. See if that helps you clear the air and get to common ground.

6. Do you love being right? Do you love being happy? (You can't always be both. When given the choice, pick happy.)

woo #2

LET IT
flow

LIKE pooping, flow is a bit of a paradox. You can't force it—you have to relax and stop pushing or trying to force movement. To enter a state of flow, you will have to stop trying so hard to be successful, happy, fulfilled and peaceful. Let go of all that crap, and just be you.

Before you can actually find your most productive and most creative state of existence, you have to stop trying. This doesn't mean that you won't have to put forth energy into your endeavors. In fact, when you are being yourself, your real self (not the self you tried to be at your high school reunion), you will put forth exponentially more energy into your dreams—because you will have exponentially more energy at your fingertips.

You will actually be able to hyperfocus your energy when you are in a state of flow. That hyperfocus is how you bring your dreams into reality. It is exhilarating!

The Tao Te Ching explains that when you are in complete harmony with the Tao (The Way/Universe), you don't have to try at all. When you are acting, thinking and behaving in a completely natural and authentic way, you are considered to be Wu Wei. You weren't meant to live a life of contrived and convoluted striving. You were meant to live your life simply and genuinely. You are who you are and when you are who you are, life is uncomplicated and effortless. It opens up like a lotus blossom to the endless blue sky.

or like a booty after taco tuesday.

The problem is, we all too often forget who we really are and try to live someone else's life. It happens all the time. Even to some of the most authentic people we know. But that's okay. You just commit to being yourself and recommit if you forget.

This state of effortless being is also called Wu Wei Wu (action without action). We reach this easy state by being our most essential selves. Visualize the planets revolving around the sun. They exhibit tremendous cosmic energy, yet they do not strive or try to revolve around the sun; they just do it.

It's simply a planet's nature to orbit the sun. It's a spontaneous, easy movement that is inherent to the state of being a celestial being. The same goes for human beings. You are meant to move in the direction inherent to who you are. If you can stop trying to people please and second

BE water,

MY **FRIEND.**

- BRUCE LEE

guess long enough to be who you really are, you can perform miracles. Effortlessly.

This is how your life is meant to be. Wu Wei! Find out who you are and be natural at it. When you are being real, you move toward your destiny without having to strive or fight.

Just be who you are naturally and let that energy propel you forward effortlessly forward like Venus orbiting around the sun, like Gisele strutting down the catwalk, like Justin Timberlake doing, well, anything.

Once you remember who you are, you will begin to experience more and more flow states in your life. Flow states are when your talents and your life lessons meet your opportunities and your destiny.

POO PARABLE

The Little Blue Dress That Almost Never Was

One of our most profound experiences of flow happened on our video shoot for "Girls Don't Poop." We had just cast a redheaded actress named Bethany who could look elegant on a toilet and nail a posh British accent. It was the day before the shoot and Suzy and our newly-hired Poo Creative Director, Nicole, were out shopping for Bethany's wardrobe. Suzy had fallen in love with a certain color blue to complement Bethany's red hair. The only problem: It was fall, and this vibrant blue was nowhere to be found. Nowhere. Suzy was considering canceling the shoot—seriously. We had nothing for Bethany to wear.

Then, at 7 p.m. the night before the shoot, Nicole said, "Well, I could make the dress..."

Suzy, who had only been working with Nicole for a couple of months, asked her, "Wait, you're just going to sew a dress from scratch? You can do that?!" And Nicole was like, "Yeah, my grandmother taught me. I made all my dance dresses in school. I mean, it will take all night, but I can do it."

So, after Nicole showed Suzy photos of the dresses she had crafted (*pictures or it didn't happen, right?*), they went to the fabric store. They found the perfect blue fabric and borrowed a sewing machine. Nicole stayed up all night sewing Bethany's dress for the shoot the next day. In fact, Nicole finished hemming the skirt just in time for the shoot's call time. When Bethany stepped into the dress, it fit her like a glove. It was magic. At that moment, our brand's spokesperson came to life. The blue dress. The red upsweep. The cheeky British accent. A Poo Princess was born.

What Suzy hadn't known about Nicole was that she was, among other things, a seamstress. What are the odds that this new 20-something Creative Director Suzy had hired was able to solve the exact creative problem at the exact time she needed her?

SUZY SAYS:
Meet yourself where you are and *miracles can happen.*

Seriously, how many young people can design and sew a dress these days? This is the epitome of flow. Nicole's unique gifts and talents were met at the exact moment with a challenge that she had been (unknowingly) training for all her life. Suzy had no idea that Nicole would be able to solve this problem when she hired her. All Suzy had was her gut telling her in the job interview that Nicole would be the perfect person to lead her creative department. So Suzy went with her gut and placed Nicole on a course to be who she was meant to be, and things have creatively fallen into place for our brand ever since.

So how will you know when your unique talents are meeting the moment of perfect challenge? Scientists have actually spent a lot of time studying this. So have ancient philosophers.

Flow is that feeling you get when you are totally engrossed—doing without doing. Ancient texts like The Bhagavad Gita describe this state of flow in detail.

In recent decades, Hungarian psychologist Mihály Csíkszentmihályi's life work has been researching this flow state in athletes, artists and scientists. He wrote an amazing book about this. It was entitled—you guessed it—*flow*. After years of painstaking research Mihály Csíkszentmihályi (pronounced "Me-high Cheek-sent-me-high"—say that 5 times fast) delineated some simple markers to help us identify when we are in flow.

Well, this page is awkward. Just turn the page to get to the exercise from the guy whose name we just mentioned but can't pronounce...

TAKE A SHIFT
exercise

Here are a few questions that will help you know if you're *in flow*.

1.
When you do this thing, can you only concentrate on the present moment and the task at hand? Are you engrossed?

2.
Do you merge your awareness with your action? Are you becoming one with the action?

3.
Do you lose all self-consciousness? Do you stop worrying about how you look or how you are doing?

4.
Do you feel your personal control over the situation? Do you feel the mastery?

5.
Is your experience of time altered? Does time pass like the seasons or zip by like a hummingbird?

6.
Do you find that whatever you are doing is intrinsically rewarding? Do you love doing it for its own sake? Does it feed your soul?

If your answer is "*yes*" to all six sets of questions, then (congrats!) you are **in flow.**

If the answer is "*no*" to any one, then you are **not in flow**. So, keep trying. Existence should be, if nothing else, a joyful pursuit of as many flow experiences as you can fit into one lifetime.

WOO #3

THE
universe
HAS YOUR
BACKSIDE

THE world wants you to succeed. Honestly, it does. This may seem counterintuitive to you, but most people you meet actually want you to make it. They want you to follow your dreams and be successful—and they actually want to help you. Why? Because when they see you doing epic shit, it inspires them—and they know what goes around comes around. We are all connected. In our hiney of hineys, we all know this. We know that, as John F. Kennedy observed, a rising tide truly lifts all boats.

There are a lot of stories we can tell ourselves about how business is a dog-eat-dog world and some dastardly character from *The Devil Wears Prada* is just waiting to snatch our nascent ideas or kill our company. Yes, this does happen. But don't focus on that and get distracted.

Turn your cheeks from the bad and, instead, choose to focus on the good. Believe all of the under-told stories of the people who give a shit. They are everywhere. There are more of those people out there waiting to be your friend—to help you. These stories just don't snatch the headlines. But these stories are the rule. So follow them instead.

We know this because our customers have saved our asses more times than we'd like to admit. Our customers have shown us a level of love and support that, quite frankly, has been astonishing. 99.9% of our customers, like 99.9% of people, actually have a lot of love in their hearts. And when given a chance to share it, they share it in ways that will put tears in your eyes. Like watching *The Notebook* while chopping onions tears.

POO PARABLE

That Time We Almost Went Out of Business

In 2013, when Poo-Pourri's business had just blown up far bigger than we'd ever imagined, we found ourselves in quite a shitstorm. After the launch of our viral video "Girls Don't Poop," we were flooded with so many orders that we ran out of product, our website kept crashing and we literally had to sleep on bubble wrap at the office just to get shipments out.

While this might sound like a good problem to have, it was a blessing that threatened to sink our young company. You see, we suddenly found ourselves with over four months in back orders, completely out of sprayers and extremely understaffed. We were in danger of pissing off every one of our new customers, not to mention permanently crashing our supply chain and disrupting our cash flow.

You see, Poo~Pourri is a secret blend of essential oils and its application requires a very, very specific sprayer. Because we hadn't really foreseen what a viral video would do for our business, we ran out of these very, very specific sprayers. And our manufacturers were completely sold out. Suzy even called the CEO of one of our suppliers. And while he said he wanted to help, he was dealing with supply chain issues of his own. He had even bigger fish to fry. There would be no sprayers for us for months.

Suzy was now facing the fact that she might have to shut down her company because we had blown through a year's worth of inventory in a matter of days. Without sprayers, we had no way to make more product. To top things off, we'd have to refund millions of dollars of online orders that our amazing video had just provided us with. Our sudden success was poised to drown and flush us.

Suzy knew this was a *doo*-or-die moment for herself and her company.

That night, Suzy couldn't sleep. She tossed and turned, thoughts of doom circling her head like buzzards. She was worried not just for her immediate family, but for her Poo family. Her little company had grown to support people's careers and lives. What would happen to the Poo Crew if we couldn't get sprayers?

The worries got so loud that Suzy got out of bed to meditate and quiet her mind. As she sat cross-legged, she got a download: Take the Sprayer CEO at his word. After all, he did say he wanted to help her. He just couldn't figure out how. Go meet him face to face; he would see a real-live person across from him, and she would help him help her. And that's exactly what Suzy did.

That morning, Suzy messaged the Sprayer CEO and told him that she had just bought a ticket to come see him. She told him that if he could tell her "no" to her face, she would go away, but she was certain he wouldn't. He didn't message her back. Regardless, Suzy went to the airport, determined. As she sat waiting to board the plane, her cell phone rang from the area code of the sprayer manufacturer.

It was the Sprayer company's VP of North America. He was calling to tell Suzy not to get on the plane. He said that the Sprayer CEO was on vacation, but had been so moved by her story that he was going to figure out how to help her. In fact, the VP who had just heard of Poo-Pourri's plight stood up in a board meeting, demanding that they figure out how to help us. "If we can't help the little guy, what are we in business for?" he asked.

The VP got creative and looked at his manufacturing overflow. He figured out a way to peel off sprayers one by one from these massive runs and

SUZY SAYS:
You have a large *cheering section* in your fellow human beings.

RELAX.
EVERYTHING IS
running

RIGHT

ON

schedule.

- THE UNIVERSE

provide them to Poo~Pourri. It would be a trickle of supplies, but it was enough oxygen to keep Poo~Pourri alive.

With this one amazingly creative and generous gesture, the Sprayer CEO and his vice president saved Suzy and the company. Their creativity and kindness allowed us to fill all of our back orders and continue to sell Poo~Pourri. This moment of human kindness has created so many jobs and prosperity in the world. Even years later, we can point back to this as a pivotal moment in the growth of our company.

To this day, we believe the Sprayer CEO and VP were working as not-so-secret agents on behalf of a supportive, loving Universe. Their small act of kindness was no small act at all—just like the thousands of customers who also refused refunds from us at this time and told us they would simply wait for us to get them their Poo~Pourri, even if it took months. This much love from strangers is humbling.

we stand on the shoulders of friendly, loving, pooping giants.

So today, Poo~Pourri works on behalf of the Universe as well. As a company, we work to bring change and transformation to those seeking it. For the one in three people in the world without access to proper sanitation, we work with the World Toilet Organization to build toilets for school kids so they can get an education and change their communities. We have donated 100% of our online proceeds for a weekend to the National Coalition Against Domestic Violence, a cause close to Suzy's heart. On International Women's Day, we raised over $30,000 for Lotus Outreach International to help educate girls in Cambodia so they can rewrite their futures away from human trafficking and poverty.

We don't mention these things to brag. We mention them because we can, each and every one of us, offer kindness. We can all be not-so-secret agents on behalf of a loving and supportive Universe. We can all help each other. We can all be someone's Sprayer CEO.

we can all give a shit. a big shit.

So who have you asked for help to achieve your dreams? There is a Sprayer CEO out there ready to help you. What unique gifts can you offer to someone to help them achieve their dreams? Would you be brave enough to call them and offer your help?

TAKE A SHIFT
exercise

Being a secret agent on behalf of the Universe is easy.
Here are *ten* life hacks that are fun and easy ways
to help the Universe along.

1.

Smile at friends and strangers alike. A smile is the world's simplest,
most valuable asset. Give it and you'll get it back.

2.

Find an errant shopping cart in a parking lot and
put it up so it doesn't ding someone's car.

3.

Find a plastic cup or straw on the ground
and take it to a recycling bin.

4.

Flirt with an elderly person. Compliment their hair
or their sweater. Ask them about their day.

5.

Let a family with kids, or someone who seems like they're in a hurry,
cut in line before you at the airport or the grocery store.

6.

Let the other person have the parking spot,
even though you saw it first.

7.

When sitting in traffic, let the person in—even if they don't
have their blinker on and they look like a jerk face.

8.

Over-tip waiters and hotel maids. Do this a lot.

9.

Do a funny dance in front of a security camera. Someone somewhere is
watching this in a lonely room.

10.

Turn off the lights when you aren't using them or aren't in the room.
It actually saves water AND electricity.

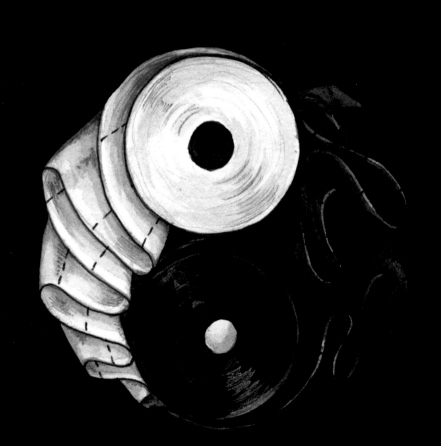

DOO
IT ON
purpose

O it on purpose. In other words, do not slide into life. Set an intention and commit to it. Your intentions are the rudders of your life. Where you set your intentions determines where life takes you.

It may sound simple, but for whatever reason, humans seem to struggle with this concept. A lot of people go through life unintentionally— half-asleep, half-awake. You wouldn't drive your car in this state, so why would you drive your life like this?

Sadly, many of us go through life yawning and complaining. We don't consciously decide things. We just let life happen. And this can make us feel like victims of circumstance, not masters of our own destiny.

We see it all around us. Couples move in together. And because it's easier to get married than to break up, we slide into tying the knot with Mr. or Ms. Good Enough at an Instagram-worthy wedding (that we can't actually afford).

We do this in all areas of our lives. We stay in jobs that bore us to death or that we don't believe in or that we might even hate. We say "yes" to going out when we really just want to stay home in our underwear. We semi-commit to health plans and wonder why our jeans are still too tight. We reluctantly choose college majors and then feel lost upon graduation. We talk about writing the next great American novel but flush our time away on Facebook.

Life on autopilot leads us into half-assed agreements we never really agreed to in the first place. The problem is we never disagreed with them either. Life just seems to happen. And many of us are left wondering why we don't feel anything that remotely resembles joy or fulfillment. Some people feel bullied by life, left nursing emotional wounds. They spend thousands of dollars and heartbeats on addictions, online shopping and crazy-making.

don't be one of these people.

Move into every stage of your life deliberately. Studies show you will be happier with the outcome if you honor life's milestones with well-thought-out decisions. Move into life not because it is "the next step that everyone else is taking." Say "yes" because you decided to. Don't yearn for a wedding or a job or even a puppy that looks social media perfect. Build a life that's right for you—one that's unfiltered and doesn't require the "likes" of your e-friends. Decide to be who you want to be by making hard decisions based on your soul's purpose. "No" is a great answer sometimes. Not every job offer will be for you. Not every opened door should be entered. Not every jelly donut should be eaten. Say "no" when you mean it. Say "yes" when you do.

FIND OUT
WHO
you are

AND
DO IT
on purpose.

- DOLLY PARTON

When we slide into things instead of deliberately stepping into our destiny, we are giving up our power. Someone else will be taking the steering wheel of your life, and that never works long term—be that a spouse, a boss, a job, an illness or even your cat. In fact, it's going to end in a crash. So grab the wheel and choose where you're going.

Sliding into things is never a good thing. Take it from people who deal with poop on a daily basis. You don't want to slide into shit.

POO PARABLE

That Time Suzy Took Us to Hawaii to Write A Song and We Sort of Didn't, But Then We Did.

Work at Poo-Pourri and you'll soon learn that Suzy loves to take us to fantastic locales to concept epic ideas.

In fact, our video, *Girls Don't Poop*, was concepted in a ski cabin in Sundance, Utah amongst the snow drifts and the glistening aspens. Suzy's taken our teams to Tulum to rethink Father's Day. She's taken

us to the cobblestone streets of Copenhagen to find inspiration for our bottle. And there was this one time when Suzy was so obsessed with creating a song that she took us to Hawaii to write it.

It was glorious. Palm trees. Azure water. Fresh Mangos (oh my gerd the mangos). We Instagrammed bottles of

Poo-Pourri on the beach. A lot. We put flowers in our hair. We ate fish right out of the ocean.

But the one thing we did *not* do was write a song.

We just somehow couldn't. We were scared. We'd never written a song before. We weren't people who wrote songs—that's what Pharrell Williams and Taylor Swift do.

But Suzy was undeterred. She could see it. She could feel it. She got chills when she thought about it (a big sign you're on to something, BTW). One morning, when everyone was completely bummed that no song had been written, Suzy came down to boost everyone's morale. Somewhere within the pep talk Suzy was giving that morning,

she just blurted out, "Imagine Where Can Go! Imagine what we can do with Poo-Pourri!" And then, suddenly—as if by magic—the chorus was born.

Suzy just sort of ...pooped it out.

And from there, the creative team knew where to go. They left the island with ten pages of lyric ideas and the same intention that Suzy had been holding all along.

One month later, Suzy was in L.A. recording an episode of *To Tell The Truth*, and one of the show's producers introduced her to Jeff Lewis. Turns out Jeff Lewis is a badass songwriter and he offered to help Suzy. So Suzy connected our VP of Creative, Nicole, with Jeff and his

SUZY SAYS:
If you aren't making a decision for yourself, *someone else is.*

producing partner, "Oh, Hush!"

Together the three of them produced a pop song that NPR has called "the next generation of jingles." Seriously, NPR.

Suzy held *so* faithfully to her intention that miracles sprang forth just when we needed them.

Likewise, Suzy knew that *Imagine Where You Can Go* was not just a song, but a music video. Yep, Suzy wanted to create a No. 1 music video about going No. 2 with Poo-Pourri. And she wanted it to be on the level of Beyoncé and Bruno Mars.

Just so happens that our new VP of Marketing, Will Clarke, was friends with a film rep who just so happens to represent Cameron Duddy, the very director of Bruno Mars' music videos. So Will set up a call with Cameron. It was love at first meeting. One choreographer, sixteen dancers, four actors and one *really* huge toilet later, an epic music video was born.

Boom!
Intention, meet Reality.

Now, we don't tell this story to brag (well, maybe just a little bit, but we did write a catchy pop song and we really weren't sure if we could). We tell it to show the power of doing things on purpose. Suzy set her intention. She visualized it. And she recommitted to it, even when things might have appeared hopeless. It truly was amazing. You should try it sometime!

Watch "Imagine Where You Can Go" on YouTube.com/Poo

Be deliberate. Be conscious of what you are doing. Be mindful of who you want to be and who you are with. Be grateful for where you are and what you have. Be loving to those around you.

be on purpose.

Then, you will find The Woo of Poo magically working for you. You will start being in the right place at the right time. You will find that you will be working toward something you love and that you will be working on building a love that you've always dreamed of.

But first you have to decide. You have to take the wheel of your own life and consciously turn down the roads less traveled. If that's what you're into.

Here's a quick litmus test that will help you be more decisive and more deliberate in your intentions: If your answer to any question or opportunity isn't a "hell yes!" then it's a "hell no!" Let that be your new motto—or maybe your next tattoo.

Don't kinda-sorta-maybe-ish want to do it. Commit. Choose one simple action step toward what you want. Date-stamp it with a by-when, and DOO it. Then choose the next simple step. Repeat.

Make conscious decisions based on who you really are, and they will change things in ways you can't even imagine.

take a shift
EXERCISE

How to set an *intention*.

1.

Grab a purple marker *(the color of your sixth chakra—your third eye!)* and draw the flower on the right on a piece of paper. Now, take the purple marker and color in the petals where you feel there is something lacking in your life—*even if it's something small*—like feeling tired and blah, or missing a friend, or those twenty pounds you need to lose because your doctor said so. If things aren't how you want them to be in this area of your life, lovingly color in the corresponding petal with purple. Let your third eye look at these aspects of your life and give you a vision for change. Listen to your intuition. Ask your highest good for clarity.

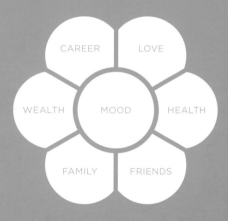

CAREER LOVE WEALTH MOOD HEALTH FAMILY FRIENDS

Now notice how you feel and where you feel it. Really sit with your flower and its purple petals. It's okay if all the petals are purple. It's okay if all petals are white. Really feel into your flower, your life, and ask why you colored in certain portions.

2.

Now that you've identified what's lacking, you've uncovered places where you can set a new intention. If you need a new job, need to pay off your student loan, want to get out of a funk with a family member, or change any part of your life, it all starts with *setting an intention*.

So, on the same sheet of paper that your drew your flower, use concise positive words to craft your new intention. For example:

I am magnetizing new friends into my life. I vibrate with joy and health. I radiate strength and compassion. I generate prosperity and tranquility. I sensualize my Tesla into existance. I nourish my body into vital longevity. I harmonize with my soulmate.

Use positive, present tense verbs that excite you and that make you tingle all over, like *reverberate, blaze, illuminate, birth, flow, synthesize, catalyze and attract.*

3.

Now visualize. Close your eyes and get comfortable. Clear your mind and *see* what your world will be once this intention becomes reality. Really be specific. *See* it. *Feel* it. *Smell* it. Your mind doesn't know what this new reality will be, so be specific with your visualization. Trust us. You have to *see it* to *be it!*

4.

Attach a feeling to this vision. *Joy. Hope. Calm. Strength. Warmth. Love. Pride. Courage.* What feelings can you wrap around this meditation that would really make this *feel* real?

5.

Open your eyes and live your life. Keep your attention on your intention, so that you know where you are going when you have to make decisions or when the universe gives you a pop quiz. Hold on to the feeling and the vision and life will change in *so* many unexpected ways.

GO
there

THEY say you talk to your friends about sex—and your best friends about poop. These friends are like family. These friends we can trust to "go there" with us. These friends have our backsides.

We suspect that's why working at Poo~Pourri feels so much like being part of a big, crazy family.

we talk about pooping. * ⁺

all. the. time.

We even get so carried away that sometimes we forget people outside of the company don't do this. After all, why should anyone be embarrassed to talk about a completely natural part of our amazing digestive process?

We know that most of the world doesn't see pooping like we do. And truth be told, poop stinks for a scientific reason. We aren't fecophiliacs at Poo~Pourri. We just aren't big on shame. In fact, we know all too well how much pinching a loaf in a shared restroom terrifies people—we used to be those people. We know the deep-seated humiliation that most people feel about stinking up a public toilet. And we know this shame can go all the way back to your toilet training as a little kid. That's why Suzy created Poo~Pourri.

Hey, before working at Poo~Pourri, many of us had hiney hangups. Boy, did we have hangups. At our old jobs in Corporate America, many of us had elaborate tricks and routines to avoid our officemates knowing we had to poop. We'd sneak into restrooms on other floors, sometimes other buildings. We'd disappear for hours at a time to go to gas stations or Starbucks. We'd spend our days strategizing, agonizing and holding it in.

Some of us would lift our feet so our coworkers couldn't recognize our shoes and attach them to the smells and noises coming from our stall, while others would sit on the toilet, unable to release the kraken until the coast was clear. All the while our precious workdays were slipping away from us. Many of us would just avoid pooping all together. We'd hold it in for hours, days even. We'd become constipated. We'd get hemorrhoids. We'd get sick. Our fecal fears were now affecting our workplace productivity and our health.

Thank the porcelain gods we found Poo~Pourri. And now we are on a mission to make sure everyone feels as comfortable pottying like a rock star at work, on dates, at the dentist's office and in other people's homes as we do.

That's because holding it in is so unbelievably bad for you. Studies have shown it can even lead to colorectal cancer. Chronically holding in your feces can lead to pelvic floor dyssynergia. This means your pelvic floor muscles, the ones you need to take a dump, basically become locked up and uncoordinated. They stop functioning normally and make it harder for you to go when you really, really need to. This is a disorder that often affects adolescent girls who are afraid and embarrassed to use the bathroom at school. And it's making them sick, both physically and emotionally.

That's why we challenge this poo taboo with our advertisements and videos. We use humor to go there and take the sting out of it—to tackle this oppressive notion that girls are too delicate, too ladylike, too bound up by whalebone corsets to need to poop.

like the book says: everybody poops.

Your boss has filed the porcelain paperwork at the office. That hottie you met on Tinder has dropped it like it's real hot while on a date. Mark Zuckerberg has had to download a brownload in the executive toilets at Facebook. Gisele Bündchen has taken a superdump in a public restroom before strutting down a runway. Samuel L. Jackson has birthed a snake on a plane.

If you have a properly functioning fanny, you poop. So let's all collectively just get over it. Cool? Cool.

There should be no shame in your bathroom game. Like Nike says, "Just do it!" Pooping anywhere you need to and in sanitary conditions is about equality and freedom.

This is the power of "going there." Challenging taboos and speaking up frees us from the shackles of cultural mores meant to hold us all down, to make us feel less than. Taboos that "shit shame" people serve no one. Taboos about girls pooping shouldn't be tolerated. Taboos about going number two at work are costing us millions in corporate profits and healthcare dollars. And all the while, this issue has been hidden under a smelly old quilt of silence, embarrassment and even misogyny.

We go there to make a point. We are doing it to get your attention. We have made it our mission to defy all of these taboos, and then some. We transform the bathroom experience with natural essential oils that trap the odor before it can escape, and this liberates people to GO anywhere. Likewise, we have created a brand that actually makes it fun to talk about poop. Because once you can talk about something and laugh at it, it no longer has any real power over you. You can see the taboo for what it is: silly, pooposterous, loodicrous, absturd...okay, we'll stop.

SUZY SAYS:
Defy.
Liberate.
Transform.
repeat.

It's a pretty awesome gig if you think about it. But we also recognize that "going there" is a journey. People's comfort levels with pooping are on a spectrum—from sphincter-clenching fear to rip-roaring, let-it-go pride. So we honor all of those experiences, and we want you to as well.

THOSE WHO ARE
EASILY
SHOCKED

SHOULD
be shocked
MORE OFTEN.

- MAE WEST

TAKE A
SHIFT
exercise

Here are some tips to help you
"go there."

1.

CHALLENGE *taboos*

What beliefs are holding you back? Now how can you challenge them? Can you exaggerate them? Sometimes ridiculous exaggeration (like an elegant British lady sitting on a toilet using outrageous potty language while she takes a dump) can help us see how silly certain taboos really are. Humor somehow sucks all the fear out of things. So what taboo do you fear most? How is it holding you back? How can you defy it? Transform it? Liberate yourself from it? Laugh at it? Turn it into a joke?

2.

BE THE *first* TO TALK ABOUT IT

Be the first to welcome someone into a room. Be the first one to speak the truth. Be the first to stand up for the oppressed. Be the first to be open about the vulnerability everyone feels about pooping at work and in public. The taboo can't be broken until someone is brave enough to be the first to speak up. So be the first.
It feels almost as good as taking a number two.

3.

SHARE *love,* NOT *odor*

Spring for a few bottles of Poo-Pourri for your employees, coworkers and for yourself. Make your bathroom (and talking about poo) a welcoming space. Yes, we know this sounds like a shameless plug, and it is. After all, shame doesn't have a hold over us, and we love selling Poo-Pourri as much as we love using it. But for real, we get letters and emails explaining how we have changed people's public restroom experiences and their lives. From Crohn's disease and irritable bowel syndrome (IBS) patients to cancer survivors going through chemo, Poo-Pourri allows people to reclaim their dignity by allowing them to go wherever they have to without embarrassment.

4.

imagine WHERE YOU CAN GO

Once you free up your mind from the worry of taboos, you've got more mindshare to give to your dreams. Where do you want to go? Like visionary activist Caroline Casey says, "The imagination lays the tracks for the reality train." You have to dream up the path first before your train will ever come in. What are you dreaming of? Where does your imagination take you? Spend time jotting these things down. Sketch them out—with your hand, not a device. Something about writing it by hand is magical.

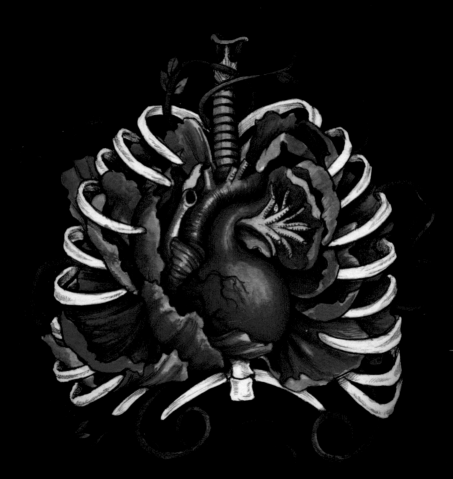

woo #6

BARE
YOUR
genius

EVERYTHING in your life that has been, and ever will be, worth doing requires that you seek it out, that you pursue it.

This is a rule of the universe: life demands pursuit.

Life wants to be chased. It wants to be embraced and lusted for. Life wants to be danced with and held tenderly. Life wants to have a sunset meal with you in Napa Valley, but first you have to woo it. It's romantic that way.

The good news is that the pursuit of what is most alive is your natural instinct. From a baby exploring the boundaries of her world by putting wooden blocks into her mouth to a teenager taking a driver's test to gain more freedom from her parents, our lives are grown from exploring the world around us, opening secret doors and becoming previously unknown versions of ourselves. Life is curious like that.

Hey, wait! Didn't curiosity kill the cat? Truth be told, curiosity set out saucers of milk for the cat. It tossed balls of yarn and used one of those red laser dot thingies to keep the cat entertained. Curiosity is the best thing to ever happen to a cat—and to you, for that matter.

So embrace your curiosity as much as possible, and then play with it like a cat does with a roll of toilet paper—pulling off every square, wondering what magic lies after the next one.

Start noticing when you feel curious. Locate the feeling in your body. Where are you feeling it? In your stomach? Your heart? What does curiosity feel like? Butterflies? Tingles down your arms? When you feel this feeling, know you are on the right track. You don't have to know what track you are on. You just need to know that following your curiosity will take you exactly where you need to go. Keep your sense of wonder intact and keep digging, following that sensation in your body.

Life's most important moments require you to seek them—to uncover them. In that way, life is just like a mystery novel and you are the detective, following your nose, your heart or your gut. You are the one dusting for prints, uncovering clues on the trail of your destiny.

Besides being a bazillion times more fun than boredom, curiosity is what will eventually lead you to your genius. This is curiosity's most important job in your life—to play matchmaker and hook you up with your genius.

genius
IS THE
RECOVERY

OF

childhood

AT WILL.

- ARTHUR RIMBAUD

And when we say "genius," we do not mean that your curiosity will lead you to meet Elon Musk or Oprah Winfrey—though that would be amazing and totally possible if you focus enough and synchronicity lines up. When we say that your curiosity will lead you to meet your genius, we mean that you possess a "genius" and that part of your job in this detective novel called Your Life is to keep reading the signs, putting the clues together and figuring out what your genius is and how you want to share it in the world. Because the world needs all of us in our genius.

What you need to know is that you (like everyone) have a special area of talent that is unique to you, and this talent is your gift, your very own superpower that will propel you into the brightest future possible.

If the pressure of the word "genius" gives you five-alarm chili heartburn, that's okay. Somewhere way back in time, the ancients got confused about what the word means. Genius used to mean a spirit guide that was sent to earth to help you develop your own particular talents. And then, over time, the word genius got mixed up with the people who possessed it. People started referring to extremely bright and talented people as geniuses. Think Marie Curie or Albert Einstein.

At this point, being a genius became an exquisitely rare and preternatural thing. Genius became the domain of historians and biographers. So discovering one's personal genius became out of reach or too egotistical to mention in polite company. It became shrouded in legend and mythology. It's a wonder anyone could ever find their own genius again.

So let's level-set: a genius is not a person.

genius is a gift that you possess.

It's not "She is a genius"; it's "She has a genius." When you uncover your
genius, and pursue it, your life will suddenly make sense
in—dare we say—magical ways.

On your path to finding your purpose and joy, a lot of people will ask you
what you're passionate about. Bless their hearts, they mean well. But like most
appetites, it changes—constantly. Passion is fleeting.

Instead, ask...

What makes you feel good?

What did you love to do at 6 or 7 years old?

What did you get in trouble for doing as a kid?

What do you do in your free time for fun?

What do you do that's so good and easy that you might even feel a little guilty
that you enjoy it so much?

Somewhere in the answers, your genius is playing hide-and-seek. Find it.
Pursue it! Chase it with all of your energy. Spend as much time in your genius
as possible.

How Suzy Tried To Slow Down

For Suzy's entire life, she was always told to slow down and be quiet. She was the kid who blurted out the answer. As an adult, she was the employee who wanted to know why it always had to be done this way, when it was so obviously not working. This got her fired—often. She was made to believe that there was something wrong with how she approached life. She was always told to be patient, to sleep on it, to put up with sluggish bureaucracy and to be less annoyed with brittle corporate structure. She tried to shore up what many people called her obvious deficits and it got her nowhere fast.

Then, she took a diagnostic test called the Kolbe A™ Index. It changed her life (for real). It showed her how she instinctively initiates work and problem solving. It made her realize that she had been wasting much of her creative energy trying to fit into a mold in which she would never fit. It was not in her nature to slow down or to be comfortable with inertia.

Everyone who works at Poo-Pourri has taken the Kolbe A Index. It has helped guide Suzy and the rest of us toward our instincts. We understand our

SUZY SAYS:

Don't try to fix what you *aren't good at.*

geniuses and how to better work with each other. We know how to put balanced teams together to optimize speed and results. The Kolbe test has helped move us to what Gay Hendricks calls "The Zone of Genius."

Take the Kolbe A for yourself at kolbe.com and check out Gay's book *The Big Leap*. Both will help you pursue the life we know you are meant to lead.

TAKE A
SHIFT
exercise

Kolbe A Mini Bathroom Quiz

Get a hint or two as to what your instincts are with this quick bathroom test inspired by the Kolbe A Index. Keep in mind that everyone has a combination of strengths, and many people fall in between the extremes.

1.

DO YOU FOLD THE TOILET PAPER OR SCRUNCH IT UP WHEN YOU WIPE?

A) I fold   **B) I scrunch**

If you fold, you might be an initiating **Follow Thru**, the kind of person who needs systems and order—the kind of person who finishes what she starts. If you scrunch, you might be the kind of person who avoids policies and procedures and starts a lot of projects but doesn't necessarily finish them.

2.

DO YOU REMEMBER TO SPRITZ POO~POURRI BEFORE YOU GO?

A) No, I forget to spritz until after I've already sat down.
(Between the legs it is).

B) I always remember to spritz the bowl before I sit.

If you're in a rush to get to the flush and forget to spray Poo-Pourri, you might be an initiating **Quick Start**—the kind of person who instigates offbeat activities and brainstorms new ideas. If you always remember to spritz the bowl, you might be the kind of person who prevents chaos, minimizes risk and finds success in sticking with what works.

3.

HOW MUCH DO YOU KNOW ABOUT YOUR POOP?

A) Everything! I look at it when I'm done. By the way, did you see that poop segment on *The Dr. Oz Show*?

B) Nothing, I do my business and get on with other things.

If you get the scoop on your poop, you might be an initiating **Fact Finder**, the kind of person who investigates, delves into data and needs information before making a decision. If you do your business and move on, you might be the kind of person who focuses on the big picture rather than the little details—the kind of person who simplifies.

4.

YOUR TOILET STOPS FLUSHING—
WHAT DO YOU DO?

**A) I take the tank lid off to start figuring
out how to fix it myself.**

B) I call the plumber.

If you construct your own environment and like to build,
fix and work with your hands, you might be an initiating
Implementor. If you rely on others to build or fix your
toilet, you might be more adept at imagining solutions
rather than physically building them.

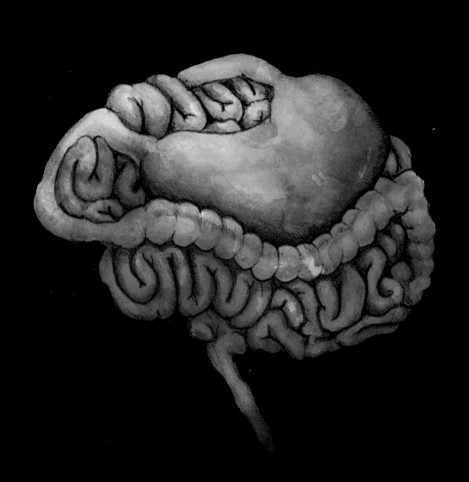

WOO #7

TRUST
YOUR *gut*

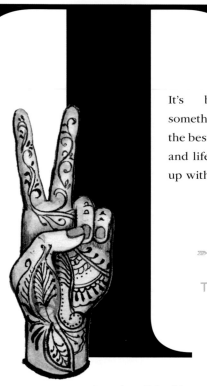

TRUST your gut. You hear this a lot. It's been said so many times, it's become something of a cliché. And while this phrase may not be the best literary device, trust your gut is the best business and life advice you'll ever get. So until someone comes up with a better way to say it, trust your effing gut!

>─◄ **POO PARABLE** ►─◄

That One Time Suzy Got A BIG Idea

Imagine this: You get this bright idea. A total light bulb moment. And this idea won't leave you alone. It follows you around like a lost puppy. It wakes you up at 2 a.m. wanting to be fed. So you tell your friends and family, "Hey, I have this idea. I think it's going to be huge. I've been making this formula with essential oils and I think I've figured out how to trap poop odor underneath the toilet water's surface."

Cue the WTF looks of judgment, confusion, disgust and doubt.

Yeah, you try telling your friends you think your next business idea involves human excrement and see how many attaboy and attagirl high-fives you get. When Suzy Batiz first had the crazy idea of Poo~Pourri, everyone either told her she was nuts or gross or a little of both. It'll never work, let alone sell, they thought.

That was—until they tried it.

And then, over time, people couldn't believe it. They couldn't live without it. Suzy knew from the beginning it would be huge. She could feel it in her gut and all over her body that she had struck upon a big, million-dollar idea. And the only evidence she had was her intuition. She had to trust her gut, even when her trusted friends and family told her it wasn't a good idea. She had to trust it enough to keep on formulating and reformulating the product. And she had to trust her gut when all she was getting were NOs from retail stores, until her first YES.

Big and new ideas are rarely recognized by people—at first. And the only way to bring the strange and powerful new thought forms into reality is to listen to your gut feelings, the same gut feelings that helped you intuit this idea to begin with. That's exactly what Suzy did, and to this day, cultivating intuition in herself and her team is one of Suzy's missions in life. After all, your gut knows a lot more than we have ever given it credit for.

THE

intuitive

MIND IS A

SACRED

GIFT

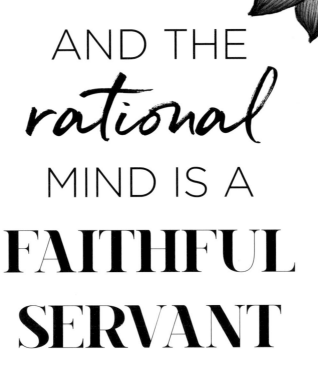

AND THE *rational* MIND IS A

FAITHFUL

SERVANT

We have created a society that **honors the servant** and has *forgotten the gift.*

- ALBERT EINSTEIN

Had Suzy not listened to her gut, we wouldn't be working here. There would be no Woo of Poo. No Poo Crew. No pooping on the job. No funny viral videos. It would stink.

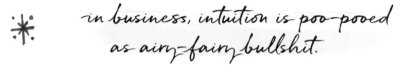

in business, intuition is poo-pooed as airy-fairy bullshit.

Banks will ask you for a business plan, not how your idea makes you feel. Investors want to see the data, not hear about the tingles you get when you talk about your vision.

Because we get this kind of reaction from people who are expected to be experts, we listen to them rather than this feeling we get deep in our bellies. Over time, many of us stop listening to our guts, and guess what? Our guts stop talking to us. We become so disconnected from our bodies and we get so inside our heads that we lose touch with a major source of divine intelligence.

So many of us are taught to listen to logic and opinion over trusting our hunches and glimmers. We follow linear thinking, education and fear. We defer to reason and argument. We go against what we instinctively know to be true. We ignore what is the right course of action. We disconnect from one of the most powerful decision-making processes that evolution has created for us.

While it's all too easy to dismiss intuition and gut feelings as New Age hocus-poocus, they're not.

There is hard science and serious investigation into how your gut is actually your second brain. It's called the enteric nervous system. This system in your gut contains over 100 million neurons and over 95% of your body's serotonin, more than your peripheral nervous system or even your spinal cord.

According to science, your gut really is a brain of sorts, and it works both independently and together with the brain inside your noggin. Your gut sends you messages all the time—and not just I-have-to-poop or why-did-you-eat-that-much messages. A large part of your emotional life is informed by the nerves in your digestive tract. Butterflies in your stomach, pits of anxiety in your abdomen and even gastric distress are all very loud and clear messages from your second brain. It's the more subtle messages we need to learn to hear—and, more importantly, accept.

Have you ever met someone new and immediately gotten a sense of who they were? Have you ever entered a room and felt deep inside that you shouldn't be there? Have you ever had a situation pan out poorly and look back in hindsight and think, "Yup, I should've listened to my gut?"

gut feelings are a real legit thing.

They are part of a scientifically validated process that involves a conversation between our two brains processing data and stimuli. In fact, bio-behavioral

SUZY SAYS: intuition not only works, it's essential to building the life you want.

scientists at the David Geffen School of Medicine at UCLA discovered that about 90% of the fibers in the primary visceral nerve, the vagus nerve, carry information from the gut to the brain and not the other way around.

This is called the brain-gut axis, and it provides constant input on the world around us. It's also how we communicate with the amazingly friendly flora in our intestines. Yep, that's right. While your mouth hole is busy eating and talking to people in the outside world, your butthole and intestines are busy talking to the microbiome that lives inside you. Fun fact: There are just as many gut bacteria cells as there are human cells in your body. (Begs the question: Who is hosting whom?)

This microbiome has evolved with us since the dawn of time. It loves us and keeps us safe, healthy and even happy. Our gut bacteria is actually essential to our health and mental well-being. This microbiome not only helps us digest our food and fight off viruses, but if the microbiome is destroyed, our bodies and lives would literally fall apart. Everything from Parkinson's disease and depression to obesity and IBS have been attributed to damaged gut flora.

*so what does this have to do
with trusting your gut?
well, everything.*

The point we are trying to make is that while something as woo-woo as your stomach talking to you like a brain may seem whackadoodle, it's actually very scientific. It's how your body works. It's science that we are just beginning to understand. The burgeoning field of neurogastroenterology is exploring these connections as we speak. New studies exploring the intricacies of our second brain emerge every day.

If you have been ignoring this body intelligence, start tapping into it... today. No time like the present! The science is there to support your exploration. Belly rumbles, butterflies and fart gurgles—these sensations truly are your second brain trying get your attention.

so, listen!

TAKE A
SHIFT
exercise

To get you started, try these tips for
listening to your gut that work and
vacation inside of you.

1.

SHUT THE *funk up*

If you are like most of us, loud thoughts swirl around and around in your brain all day like a toilet that won't stop flushing. We over-identify these thoughts. Many of us actually think we are these thoughts. We let them define us. But we shouldn't. We are not our thoughts. We are so much more. As Walt Whitman said, we contain multitudes! You are not your depression or your anxiety. You are not your to-do list or your fixation about your muffin top. These thoughts are just noisy tourists in your beautiful mind's landscape. So, find a relaxing place and go quiet your mind and kick those assholes out. Shut the funk up in your head. How? You can do this by focusing on your breath and counting. Google how to meditate. It really is that easy. Try downloading the Headspace app on your phone and practice. It takes practice, but practice makes peaceful. And once you quiet your head thoughts, you can finally hear what your gut has been discreetly telling you all along.

2.

GET OVER *feeling weird*
ABOUT FEELINGS

Our species evolved to have emotions for a reason. Listen to them. Honor them. Feel them. Don't flush them down the toilet as waste—those pipes will get backed up and overflow, trust us. Honoring your feelings is quite simple. Feel sad? Cry. Feel tired? Rest. Feel sick? Stay home and don't get the rest of us sick, you martyr. Feel stressed? Blow off some steam; go for a run. Just express yourself so it's not bottled up inside of you, creating gas bubbles. Blurt it out where no one else can hear, scream into your pillow, kick your heels onto the mattress. You get the idea—just don't aim that energy at anyone else. This is a feel-out-loud party for one: you.

It's also important to feel into which situations give you energy and which ones rob you of it. Same goes for people. Some will feed your energy level. Some will drain it. Pay attention to how your body feels. There's every class of neurotransmitter in your gut, and for that matter, your heart also receives input about the outside world; it processes stimuli and sends signals to your brain. So don't just trust what your rational mind wants you to think. Remember, you aren't just your thoughts. Trust the very intelligent feelings in your body. Search for what feels right. Put words to your feelings. Honor them. Express them. Allow them to guide you. They can take you so much further than your mind could ever think.

3.

LET *"eureka"* BE YOUR THING

Intuition arrives in epiphanies and flutters. It shows up dressed up as urges, twinges and aversions. The old you used to ignore these things. The new you, who is comfortable with The Woo of Poo, loves this shit. Let your process be led by your impressions. Your intuition will whisper in your heart at times, and at others, it will punch you in the gut. Be ready to pay attention to both.

4.

JOT DOWN YOUR *dreams*
WHEN YOU WAKE UP

Ever notice how when you eat certain foods, you have super weird dreams? Now that you're aware that there really is a brain-gut axis, this doesn't seem so hard to explain. Your gut instinct even speaks to you when you are asleep! How cool is that? So keep a dream journal by your bed and interpret those dream metaphors to better unlock your intuition. Dreams can offer guidance and insight into your career, health and relationships. Dreaming has a way of solving things that aren't so obvious to our rational mind. Got a hard problem? Try repeating the question every night for the next week before bed and see what happens. Just do us a favor: Try not to corner your coworkers by the coffeemaker, giving them long, detailed descriptions of your dreams. Nobody likes that. Nobody.

5.

TEND THE *garden* OF YOUR GUT

Antibiotics, junk foods, sugar, stress and illness can deplete the healthy strains of bacteria in your gut. Over time, this can have disastrous health and mood implications for you. So replace your lost or damaged gut flora with probiotic foods. Probiotics, like kombucha, sauerkraut, kimchi and yogurt nourish and promote your biome. These foods are cultured with the strains of healthy bacteria (look for foods or supplements with lactobacillus acidophilus and bifidobacterium lactis).

Eat foods to support a healthy gut ecosystem in which your gut bacteria can thrive. Foods like bananas, honey, onions, garlic, leeks, asparagus, oatmeal and apples are all high in fibers and nutrients that promote the increase in friendly bacteria.

6.

GET YOUR HANDS *dirty* AGAIN

Back in the day, tending vegetable gardens and flowerbeds was part of our daily chores. Kids played outside until the streetlights came on. They had grime under their fingernails from digging in the dirt. When food dropped on the ground, moms would dust it off and say "a little dirt never hurt anybody!" Now, thanks to antibacterial soap, hand gels and germ-killing wipes, we have lost our connection to the soil. Our leaky guts and intestinal disorders are all the evidence needed for some researchers to state that we are "Vitamin Dirt" deficient. With 70% of our entire immune system located in our guts and with trace minerals from dirt being so essential to keeping this ecosystem balanced and healthy, it's really no surprise that so many of us have intestinal problems. Now, we aren't saying go out and eat dirt if you have gut issues (though some experts will tell you to do just that). We do, however, recommend dirt mineral supplements like RESTORE for Gut Health to promote and support the biodiversity of your gut flora with the minerals that you are probably missing from being disconnected from the earth's soil.

7.

JUST BECAUSE IT'S *gross* DOESN'T MEAN YOU SHOULDN'T TRY IT

Ready for this? Are you sure? Okay... Fecal transplants. What is a fecal transplant? Exactly what you think. The poop of a person with healthy gut flora is injected into the butt of a person suffering from very unhealthy gut flora. This procedure is, of course, performed by licensed doctors. If someone other than a licensed doctor offers to do this to you, run! All kidding aside, fecal transplants are a medical procedure that has been known to save the lives of people with severe Crohn's disease. And as gross as it may sound, if you are one of the 45 million Americans who suffer from IBS or Crohn's, you should seriously look into the advances being made in this area of medicine. What's a little poo shared among friends when it can save your life? And as always: Doo your research first.

woo #8

KEEP
CRAP
OUT OF YOUR
mouth

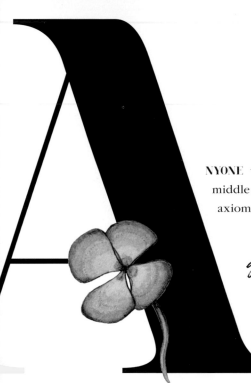

ANYONE who's lived through computer science in middle school has heard the old programming axiom:

gigo:
garbage in, garbage out.

Well, your eighth-grade teacher was right. The quality of what you put into any system directly correlates with the quality of the outcome. This is especially true regarding the food that goes into your body's system.

If you don't feed yourself good, nourishing, whole foods and take care of yourself, not only will your poop be completely gnarly and irregular, but so will your life. If you eat the food-ish substances and the fast foods that are advertised to you, if you don't take proper care of your most precious and valuable instrument (your body), you will eventually get sick. And when you are sick, you can't pursue life fully; you can't manifest the dreams that you came here to manifest.

At Poo~Pourri, since we turn crappy into happy and shitty into pretty, *gigo for us means: good in, good out.*

"Health is wealth" is not just a hippie bumper sticker on the back of a beat-up Volkswagen van. It's a truth that Suzy came to realize early on when getting Poo-Pourri off the ground as a start-up. Suzy says she realized just how important her health was after getting cold after cough after flu after stomach bug during each of our trade show seasons.

And things at Poo-Pourri were not going to slow down. So if things weren't going to slow down, Suzy was going to have to keep up. She had to train her body like an athlete does to compete. And that meant feeding herself in ways she had not been willing to do before.

Suzy committed to training her body to be strong enough to move at the speed her start-up business needed and to toughen up to handle all the germs she was encountering on her travels. She dove deep into whole foods and vegetables and cutting-edge nutritional science like pre- and probiotics. She committed to getting into the best shape of her life so she could compete and perform on the stage she was meant to be on.

This wasn't a snap of the fingers. But it wasn't so hard either. Suzy let her curiosity fuel her quest for foods and ideas that would nourish her body. She played with raw foods. She dove into family-friendly vegetarian recipes. She made her own kombucha and sriracha sauce. She revamped everything about how she approached eating. She took seriously where her food came from.

Suzy simply chose to always eat real food. To savor and enjoy it. To look at food as fuel and as medicine. Because while "garbage in, garbage out" may be true, so is "good in, good out." Healthy in, healthy out. Positive in, positive out. Nurtured in, nurtured out. Love in, love out. See how that works? Practice it and see what happens.

She added supplements and powders to her morning teas. She explored herbs, essential oils and juices. Suzy put her body and her health first. And it paid off big time for her and her skyrocketing company.

SUZY SAYS:

The only way we can manifest a healthy and transformative new world is by being healthy and *transformative individuals.*

Suzy proved that working hard and starting a business doesn't mean you have to sacrifice your health. This myth serves no one. In fact, the opposite is true. The more you focus on your personal health, the healthier your business will become. Health is wealth, truly.

At our Poo~Pourri headquarters, we are known for our walking meetings, our swopper chairs (check them out at swopperusa.com), and our healthy lunches and snacks.

suzy knows that a team runs on its stomach.

And since she saw what the law of "good in, good out" did for her, she decided to invest in supplying our team with the healthiest foods she could find. As our CEO, she committed very early on to making sure everyone at Poo~Pourri was nourished to his or her fullest pootential.

If you are going to dare to chase your dreams, to fulfill your destiny, you are going to need optimum health. So put the good in, and the good will come out. The proper watering, care and feeding of yourself has to be your first priority.

LET
FOOD
BE THY

medicine

AND

MEDICINE

BE THY

food.

- HIPPOCRATES

TAKE A
SHIFT
exercise

◄━━━━━━►━━━━━━◄

While we aren't doctors, nor do
we like diets, we do have some fun,
common-sense tips to help you get
started on fueling up for your dreams.

1. Eat a rainbow of fruits and vegetables. Fill your plate with veggies. Let meat, pastas and breads be condiments. Make it a game. Design a colorful plate of art with sweet potatoes, lettuces, yellow squash, tomatoes, Swiss chard, spinach and beets. Blueberries for dessert, anyone?

2. Healthy recipes can be amazing. Get inspired by rebarmodernfood.com and the Green Kitchen iPhone app. Follow health-based chefs on Instagram. Use fresh herbs like basil, dill, mint, tarragon and cilantro to kick simple recipes up a notch.

3. Stay away from the inside aisles at the grocery store. These aisles are typically filled with the unhealthy shit—processed foods, artificial sugars and preservatives, oh my. Instead, fill your cart with the fresh items found on the perimeter walls of the grocery store. And if you can't pronounce the ingredients on the label—stop, drop and run.

4. Eat smaller meals as you get closer to bedtime. We love this rule: Eat like a queen for breakfast, a princess for lunch and a pauper for dinner.

5. Make Saturday mornings about long walks and farmers' markets.

6. Eat out less. Split a meal when you do go out to eat. Most restaurant portions are double, triple, even quadruple a proper portion size. Better yet, learn to cook it yourself. Seriously, in less time than it takes to watch a cooking show, you could have made something nourishing and delicious for yourself.

7. If you need a snack, listen to Eve and eat the apple. If you aren't hungry enough to eat an apple instead of a less healthy snack, then you actually aren't really hungry. It's a great litmus test to keep from eating out of boredom. Keep apples and fresh fruit by your desk and bad snacks waaaaay out of reach.

8. Always be flushing your system. Water. Water. And more water. Always be drinking water. Often, when you think you're hungry, you're actually just thirsty. Also people get cranky when they need water, and you've got way too much to do to be cranky.

9. Good news in, good news out. Actively seek and binge on positive, uplifting stories. TED, Upworthy, NPR's *This American Life* and *Radiolab* are good places to start. If you can't find time to do that, then try doing a 5-day news fast. Turn off CNN and FOX. Turn off the news alerts and delete Facebook from your phone (don't worry, you can always put it back on your phone later). Give yourself a break from the constant cacophony of tragedy, outrage and amplified drama. You'll be amazed at how your stress level will improve as well as by the energy you will free up. Feeding your mind with goodness is essential.

10. Keep the verbal poo-poo out of your mouth and don't shit talk. Don't be negative. Don't beat yourself up. Don't say cruel things about other people OR yourself. Don't be a bully. Be kind and affirmative with your words in every way. Be positive with your intention. Be a yea-sayer. Spread compliments. Share appreciations. Speak of possibilities. The positive energy is infectious and it will help attract the people, projects and things you desire most on this journey. Try this: Give out three compliments a day for the next seven days straight. Like a stranger's outfit? Tell them. Coworker do a good job on a recent project? Tell them. Notice the smile just a few words can bring to someone's face and the positive shift it can bring to both of your days.

woo #9

own
YOUR
shit

AS you might have noticed by watching our videos, our Poo Princess, played by Bethany, owns her shit—literally and figuratively. She isn't afraid to talk about pooping. She isn't afraid to acknowledge the stinky truth about it either. And she isn't afraid to take control of the shituation and her health with Poo~Pourri, so she can relax and go whenever, wherever she needs to go. Sure, we do play this for laughs and for sales, but Bethany's character is really what owning your shit looks like. To many people, owning your shit might seem synonymous with fearlessness.

but owning your shit is about integrity

The Poo Princess is who she is, she does what she does, and she isn't afraid to claim it. She has integrated all the parts of herself, even the paradoxical ones that society might tell her to hide. She's beautiful and she has a potty mouth. She's elegant and she takes dumps in public restrooms. This kind of honesty is disarming because the truth is always astonishingly powerful.

Instead, somewhere along the way, we are told to compartmentalize all of the different versions of ourselves, to cover our mistakes, to hide our unflattering past and to filter our photos. We are expected to show up differently depending on the people and location. We are told to keep things in tidy little boxes to not disturb those around us. But a life full of love and purpose is sort of rangy and messy. It really doesn't grow well inside tight little boxes.

SUZY SAYS:
There is no such thing as work-life balance. Only work-life wholeness.

When we separate parts of ourselves (even the ones we might be ashamed of) into compartments, we show up smaller than we are, less powerful. Only when we integrate everything can we fully know our potential. Then we show up whole all the time. We are the same person at work, at home,

ON
PERSONAL
integrity

HANGS
HUMANITY'S
fate.

- R. BUCKMINSTER FULLER

at church, in love, in traffic and in the office. When we integrate all of our "selves" into one, we will always show up with integrity. Integrity is the end result of integrating our narratives and all of our selves into our most powerful, authentic and complete self.

owning your shit is also about accountability.

We're quick to take credit when something wonderful happens, but when something bad happens, we tend to look around for excuses or someone to blame. It's time to point in, not out, and take responsibility for what happens in your life. So many of us could win Oscars for playing the victim; we claim life happens to us. But we have 100% ownership and control of our reality.

Late to an appointment because the traffic was unusually heavy? Take responsibility. Stuck in an unhappy relationship because your partner isn't putting in the effort? Take responsibility. Project at work got dropped because your coworker didn't do his part? Take responsibility.

Assess and take ownership of what you did to cause these things to happen. Once you own your shit, you will free yourself to drive results and make changes.

POO PARABLE

One of our favorite stories about owning your shit involves Bryan, a Poo Inventory Manager. It was after a crazed fourth quarter and Bryan was doing his usual job of managing the high-velocity demands of our supply chain. In the rush of the workday, Bryan overlooked a number or two. However, this mistake, once Bryan caught it, wasn't just a number or two. It was over $20,000.

In a multimillion-dollar supply chain, hiding a $20K mistake can be done. Facts could have been shuffled around. Ex-employees could have been blamed. Spreadsheets could have been lost. But that's not what Bryan did. He wasn't one of those people who blames others for his problems or creates stories to hide behind. However, he also wasn't a person who liked making mistakes. He was kind of a numbers geek and was horrified that he had cost the company this much money.

So instead of hiding or scapegoating, Bryan owned his shit. He went to Suzy's office and told her—shaking—about his $20,000 mistake, thinking he was surely going to be punished or, worse, fired. However, the exact opposite happened. Suzy was blown away with Bryan's courage and vulnerability to come into the CEO's office and admit this. She told him that. And Bryan stood there sort of shocked that she wasn't mad. And she wasn't. She thanked him and moved on to,

"Okay, now let's get creative and fix this."

She was proud of him and wanted him to know that she would also have his back—or anyone who owned their shit like that.

It's easy to think that this worked out because Bryan works at a company that believes in owning your shit. But the fact also remains that everyone, deep down, respects people who own their shit. And regardless if Suzy had been proud of Bryan or not, he would have been able to stand tall in taking accountability, and that's what owning your shit is all about.

TAKE A
SHIFT
exercise

➤━━━━━━━◄━━━━━━━➤

The next time you want to blame
your problems on something—or
someone—else, check yo'self
with these *six* steps.

1. HEAR *yourself*

No, really. Listen to how you sound to other people. Do you hear yourself blaming people and making excuses? Are you always the victim? Are people always picking on you? Are things happening to you? Or do you take responsibility for your actions? Are you making things happen and handling the shit that comes your way? Are you aware that every event in your life, even the really shitty ones, is the result of choices you have made and are making? If not, slow down, take a look in the bathroom mirror and reframe.

2. BLAME *no one*

This is your life. If there's a problem, you're going to have to be the one to fix it. Blaming people will just slow you down and prevent change.

3. DON'T TAKE THIS *universe*, OR ANY OF ITS INHABITANTS, *personally*

No one is doing this to you. Understand the laws of physics and play by them. People slip up. Acknowledge it, readjust your game plan if needed, forgive (other people and yourself) and move on. Don't hold on to the past—it'll hold right back on to you and prevent you from moving toward your best, most positive future.

4. SEEK *feedback*

This is harder than it sounds, because you have to listen. Like, really listen. Put your phone down, make eye contact and soak in every word. A lot of time, we avoid feedback because it's not what we want to hear. It's not always compliments and gold stars. So don't get too excited about positive feedback or too hurt by negative feedback. Instead, devour feedback. It will help make you more conscious of how you are doing. It will help you better solve problems and improve your game. Feedback is the secret sauce of badassery.

5. TRY TO *understand* THE PEOPLE YOU DON'T AGREE WITH—BE THAT FAMILY, COWORKERS OR *even strangers*

It leads to insight and openness. Seek insight, not agreements, from people. Be okay with slightly uncomfortable conversations. Life is a game. Find a good coach and talented teammates who challenge you and your opinions.

6. ALWAYS BE *grateful*

Start a journal, and begin every day with gratitude. Before you even get out of bed, write down one thing you're grateful for. Be thankful for those who are willing to give you their thoughts. This took effort, time and heartbeats. Even if it's not the feedback you wanted, it's energy and knowledge, and these things are always valuable. Be thankful for the challenging times or people who taught you an important lesson. Just be thankful.

WOO #10

DO
epic
SHIT

HERE'S the truth about doing epic shit: it's not for everyone. If it was, everyone would be doing epic shit and changing the world. It's not because it has to be hard or you have to earn your stripes or any of that you-got-to-pay-your-dues-kid rubbish. Doing epic shit is actually easy when you are pursuing life, following your genius and going with the flow (see Woos #1-9). That much we've already established.

the thing is that doing epic shit is, well, scary.

And that's actually a good thing. When you are doing truly creative work, when you are making something that's never existed before or doing something that's never been done, we all tend to freak out. That's normal.

Creative acts force us to dance with the unknown, and our paleolithic DNA is terrified of this ghostly salsa partner. Our paleolithic DNA would prefer that we get a job at a big, slow, very established company with a pension plan because this means we are devoting our precious time, attention and resources to something with an assured outcome.

That's because, in cavewomen times, chasing unknown outcomes was a potentially deadly pursuit. That is why doing epic shit can sometimes feel like a raptor from jurassic park is chasing us.

Humans evolved to avoid the unknown and to seek the status quo. And that kind of risk aversion obviously worked. There are now like seven billion of us on the planet. Good job, security seekers! Being hardwired for security is normal human behavior; being an entrepreneur and working for a start-up is not. You have to be a little bit of an alien to want to do it.

And whether you are building a rocket ship to Mars or developing a Before-You-Go Toilet Spray, every act of creation involves a big, wide-eyed gulp of courage.

The good news is you might very well be one of those oddballs who have this courage. If you are, there is no question that you can do epic shit in your lifetime. This doesn't mean you won't have fear; you will have big baskets full of fear cobras, but you will charm them to sway to your music. You will just follow your visions and crazy ideas and feel the fear anyway. You will enjoy creating a life that scares the shit out of you on a daily basis.

Sometimes weirdos, like us, come together as companies and these companies create cultures that do epic shit. They change industries and dent Universes. Think of information pioneer Dame Stephanie "Steve" Shirley, Sirius XM cofounder Martine Rothblatt and Apple founder Steve Jobs. "Here's to the crazy ones," they say. "The square pegs in the round holes…"

At Poo~Pourri, doing epic shit is all about change and transformation. And change and transformation are the exact opposites of stability. The outcome is always at risk, which most human beings hate. Most human beings like sure bets.

You really have to face this fear to work at Poo~Pourri, or any other start-up, because "do epic shit" is not just another beautiful hand-lettered motto on the wall; it's both a promise and a threat. It's a standard that, if you actually live by it, will stretch and grow you like your stomach at an all-you-can-eat buffet. Do epic shit or get off the pot.

 the heat and pressure will either crush you or form you into a diamond. you choose.

There are easier ways to make a dime, but only one way to make a diamond. The question is: Do you really want that kind of heat and pressure in your life? If your answer is "yes," keep reading (also consider applying for a job at Poo~Pourri). You are likely to be one of the weirdos who likes dancing with the unknown, who enjoys the rush of scaring the crap out of yourself regularly.

fear is always going to be there when you are doing something creative.

It will manifest in many ways. It will dress up like procrastination. It will disguise itself as comfy sweat pants and lull you into binge watching all six seasons of *Lost* on Netflix. Other times, your fear will be very bold and straightforward; it will just be sitting at your workspace, naked as a panic attack. Fear is clever. You need to understand yours.

The key to doing epic shit is not to try to eliminate fear. You can't kill your fears. That just makes them bigger, scarier and Hulk-ier. You can't make them go away either. (They actually have a job to do: protecting you and keeping you alive.) You have to befriend your fears. Acknowledge them. Talk to them. Understand why they're here. And little by little, even though your fear is present, it will lose its power over you.

In fact, when fear shows up, be glad! It means you are walking into terra incognita—unknown land. You are about to do something that you've never done before. You are creating. You are changing. You are expanding.

People who practice befriending their fears and insist on doing their life's work despite being terrified often appear to the outside world to be "fearless." We work with many of these "fearless" types at Poo~Pourri. And we can tell you from firsthand experience, they feel the fear—oooh, they feel it—but they just go for it anyway. That's really the trick to doing epic shit. Feel the fear. And do it anyway. That's a book actually. You should read it.

take a shift
EXERCISE

The next time you want to blame your problems on something—or someone—else, check yo'self with these *eight* steps.

1.

If your fear were a monster, what would it look like? Give your fear a face. Draw what your fear looks like.

2.

What are the top three disguises your fear cleverly takes?

3.

When was the last time you made a decision based on fear?

4.

If you weren't afraid, what would you do?

5.

If you could be anything, what would you be?

6.

If you could go anywhere, where would you go?

7.

What scares you the most?

8.

How can you play nice with this fear monster? How can you turn the scary monster into a cuddly, harmless teddy bear?

Another mental monster keeping you from doing epic shit is fear's roommate, limited beliefs. Limited beliefs are over-zealous historians keeping note of all the stories you've told yourself as to why you can't do something. It's not possible. I've failed before. No one's ever done it before. I don't know how. It's too hard. I'm not smart enough. Blah, blah, blah. You can either let these stories write your narrative, or you can rip them to pieces like a roll of toilet paper.

At Poo~Pourri, when consultants or agencies tell us they are going to help us think "outside the box," Suzy always replies with...

"what box?"

This anything-is-possible, think-outside-this-dimension kind of problem solving is how Poo~Pourri was built. And it's this kind of thinking that you can also use to make quantum changes in your life. If you believe you can't, well, you're right. In order to change your life, you are going to have to change your limiting beliefs. That sounds easy, right? But we get very attached to our beliefs. We even get angry if people try to prove us wrong. Wars are fought over beliefs, in fact. That's why Buddhism often talks about the wisdom of emptiness. When you don't believe something is impossible, suddenly it's not.

POO PARABLE

The Epic Idea That Changed
Poo~Pourri Forever

Challenging the belief of what's possible is exactly what Suzy did when her gut told her it was time to take Poo~Pourri to the next level. It was 2013. At the time, 99% of Poo~Pourri's business was done through selling the product wholesale to retailers. PooPourri.com sold a bottle or two per day, at best. But Suzy didn't just want to gradually, safely enter the e-commerce, direct-to-consumer space; she wanted to bust through the door in an epic way—through a branded viral video.

Traditional experts and marketing consultants told Suzy that you can't intentionally make a viral video that converts into actual sales. Well, you can, and Poo~Pourri did. Suzy was one of the first people to actually pioneer this form of conversion YouTube marketing, mainly because she didn't see the same boxes that other people told her were there.

When "Girls Don't Poop" launched in 2013, our online business increased 1,300%—overnight. The ad received 10 million views in its first two weeks. We had not only broken the Internet with our video, we almost broke our company. We couldn't keep up with the insane number of orders that Suzy's vision had brought us.

Thinking outside of your dimension can change things drastically. It's disruptive. And disruption, if you do it right, always brings you a bigger share of the future. And, boy, did we get our share of the future. We had calls, emails and orders flooding into our tiny offices. We were all working 20-hour shifts. Much of the Poo Crew spent the night at the office, sleeping on bubble wrap when they needed to catch some shut-eye. It was a thrilling time for all of us, and we got to witness firsthand what it meant to truly do epic shit!

To this day, our internal team of creative thrill-seekers still pushes to go for the seemingly impossible. We'd never written a song and produced a music video before—until we did. We'd never directed our own commercials or started a production company before—until we did. We'd never written a book before—until we did.

With every level of success and change that you manifest, you will constantly have opportunities to challenge your own status quo.

like suzy, you should always ask "what box?"

What box am I putting myself in? What constraints am I agreeing to that don't have to be there? How can I think outside of this dimension?

LIFE
SHRINKS
OR
EXPANDS

IN
PROPORTION
TO ONE'S
courage.

- ANAÏS NIN

BONUS: POO PARABLE

When Life Won't Give You A Door, Make A Window

One of our favorite stories of "What box?" thinking, ironically, involves a lot of boxes. It was during the great deluge of orders after "Girls Don't Poop." Our fulfillment managers, Lisa and Brendan, were working night and day to get orders out. However, the fulfillment center and the warehouse were in two separate, neighboring offices. So they would have to dolly product and boxes back and forth between the two adjacent offices, over and over again.

Lisa had an idea to make this process work faster. It was simple: Let's just put a door in the wall between the warehouse and the fulfillment center. Then, we could pass the inventory through the door and speed it out of the fulfillment center onto the shipping trucks. This could speed things up exponentially.

Only problem: Our landlord gave us the Heisman and said "no." We were not allowed to build a door in the wall. Days and nights went by with Lisa and Brendan breaking their backs, dollying tons of boxes of Poo~Pourri out of the warehouse door, around the sidewalk and pulling them up the ramp into the fulfillment center on repeat. Talk about Déjà Poo.

One morning, at around 2 a.m. (when most great ideas come), Brendan had a thought! The landlord said no door, but what about a window? They got the okay, and Brendan got a sledgehammer. He made a window between the warehouse and the fulfillment center through which his team was able to pass the boxes of product. This allowed the team to get all the orders filled 10 times faster than lugging the boxes on the dolly.

in life, there are going to be walls.

There are going to be times when you know you need to build a door to get to the other side, and people and circumstances are going to tell you "no," you can't build a door. And you are just going to have to bust out your sledgehammer and make a window instead.

Stability is easy. Certainty is nice. Routines are safe. Because of this, the thought of breaking through those walls of comfort to the other side can be scary. Don't let it be.

"Change is hard" is a box you can't grow in. So ignore that box because, guess what, it isn't real anyway. Change is change. How you perceive it is really up to you.

If you can learn to love chasing the change, if you can master this Woo, you can grow yourself out of any Poo.

so, what are you waiting for?

let's

SUZY batiz

Suzy Batiz is the inventor, founder and CEO of Poo~Pourri. A serial entrepreneur and believer in magic, Suzy created her exponentially growing multimillion-dollar enterprise without borrowing a dime or enlisting a single investor.

She did this practicing a method that she calls the Radical Resonance System™—a body wisdom method that combines somatic training, quantum physics and interpersonal evolutionary processes. Today, Suzy teaches other entrepreneurs how to follow what's alive through resonance and continues to nurture her company as a top place to work, play and profit for dozens of employees she lovingly calls her "Poo Crew."

Suzy's been profiled in *Forbes*, featured on CNBC and honored by Ernst & Young and Inc. 5000 as a Top Entrepreneur. Her next book, *Radical Resonance*, will be out soon, so stay in touch with her on

 SUZYBATIZ.COM

THE
poo
CREW

The Poo Crew is a super squad of some of the smartest, kindest, weirdest, funniest and hardest-working people on the planet. Our collective mission is to change the way the world thinks about the things they've always done—

one liberating poop at a time.

If our products, videos, emails, jokes, customer care or THIS BOOK (!!!) have ever made your day a little bit brighter, we'd love for you to make *our day* by letting us know!

EMAIL US:
PooLove@PooPourri.com

TALK CRAP WITH US ON SOCIAL:
@PooPourri   #PooPourri

LEAVE US A REVIEW:
PooPourri.com